Planet Saturn

ANN O. SQUIRE

Children's Press®
An Imprint of Scholastic Inc.
New York Toronto London Auckland Sydney
Mexico City New Delhi Hong Kong
Danbury, Connecticut

Content Consultant
Bryan C. Dunne
Assistant Chair, Assistant Professor, Department of Astronomy
University of Illinois at Urbana–Champaign
Urbana, Illinois

Library of Congress Cataloging-in-Publication Data
Squire, Ann, author.
 Planet Saturn / Ann O. Squire.
  pages cm. — (A true book)
 Audience: 9 to 12.
 Audience: Grades 4 to 6.
 Includes bibliographical references and index.
 ISBN 978-0-531-21156-4 (lib. bdg.) — ISBN 978-0-531-25362-5 (pbk.)
 1. Saturn (Planet)—Juvenile literature. I. Title. II. Series: True book.
 QB671.S68 2014
 523.46—dc23   2013024334

All rights reserved. Published in 2014 by Children's Press, an imprint of Scholastic Inc.
Printed in China 62
SCHOLASTIC, CHILDREN'S PRESS, A TRUE BOOK™, and associated logos are trademarks and/or registered trademarks of Scholastic Inc.

1 2 3 4 5 6 7 8 9 10 R 23 22 21 20 19 18 17 16 15 14

**Front cover: The *Cassini*
spacecraft flying by Saturn**

**Back cover: The *Huygens* spacecraft
on Saturn's moon Titan**

Find the Truth!

Everything you are about to read is true *except* for one of the sentences on this page.

Which one is **TRUE**?

T or F Saturn's moon Titan is the largest moon in the solar system.

T or F A year on Saturn is much longer than a year on Earth.

Find the answers in this book.

Contents

THE BIG TRUTH!

Disappearing Rings

The colors in this photo are enhanced to show different layers of clouds on Saturn.

Scientists did not see Saturn's rings until the invention of telescopes.

The *Voyager 2* spacecraft took this close-up photograph of Saturn in 1981.

CHAPTER 1

The Ringed Planet

At an average distance of 800 million miles (1.3 billion kilometers) from Earth, Saturn is the farthest **planet** that can be seen without a telescope. To the naked eye, Saturn looks like a bright star in the night sky. If you do have a telescope, though, you will see a lot more. You can spot Saturn's rings with even the simplest telescope. Saturn is not the only planet with rings. But it is the only one whose rings are so large, beautiful, and easy to see.

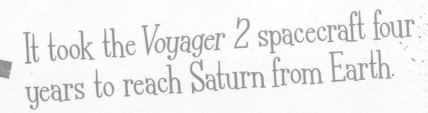

It took the Voyager 2 spacecraft four years to reach Saturn from Earth.

Saturn in the Solar System

Saturn is one of the eight planets in our solar system that **orbit** the sun. Saturn is the sixth planet from the sun. It is the second largest of all the planets, after Jupiter. Because it is so far from the sun, Saturn is considered one of the outer planets. The other outer planets are Jupiter, Uranus, and Neptune. The inner planets, or those closest to the sun, are Mercury, Venus, Earth, and Mars.

Saturn and the other outer planets are much larger than the inner planets.

Mercury Earth   Jupiter   Saturn   Uranus

Venus Mars

Neptune

Sun

Venus

Saturn

Saturn can sometimes be seen in the sky with the naked eye. This photo also includes Earth's neighbor planet, Venus.

From Saturn to Earth

Both Saturn and Earth orbit the sun. They both also follow slightly **elliptical** paths. Sometimes the two planets are on the same side of the sun. Sometimes they are on opposite sides. As a result, the distance between them changes a lot. At their closest point, Saturn and Earth are 746 million miles (1.2 billion km) apart. When they are farthest apart, the distance is more than 1 billion miles (1.6 billion km).

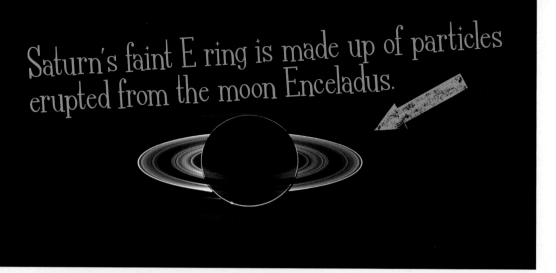

Saturn's faint E ring is made up of particles erupted from the moon Enceladus.

Saturn's hazy outer E ring is easiest to see from the side of Saturn facing away from the sun.

Saturn to the Sun

Because its orbit is an ellipse, Saturn's distance to the sun also changes. The closest point to the sun is called the perihelion. For Saturn, this is 839 million miles (1.4 billion km). The farthest distance is the aphelion. At this point, Saturn is 934 million miles (1.5 billion kilometers) from the sun. Saturn is more than nine times farther from the sun than Earth is. As a result, the tops of the clouds at Saturn's surface remain chilly all year long.

A Huge Planet

Saturn is an enormous planet. It measures more than 74,500 miles (120,000 km) from side to side. Saturn is more than nine times as wide as Earth. It would take 760 Earths to fill the space occupied by Saturn. If Earth were the size of a gumball, Saturn would be as big as a soccer ball.

Saturn is the second-widest planet in our solar system. Earth is the fifth widest.

EARTH

SATURN

A Lightweight Planet

Despite its large size, Saturn is a real lightweight. It is the least **dense** planet in the solar system. Earth is the densest planet. Its average density is eight times that of Saturn. If it were possible to drop Saturn into a giant pool of water, this light planet would float on top!

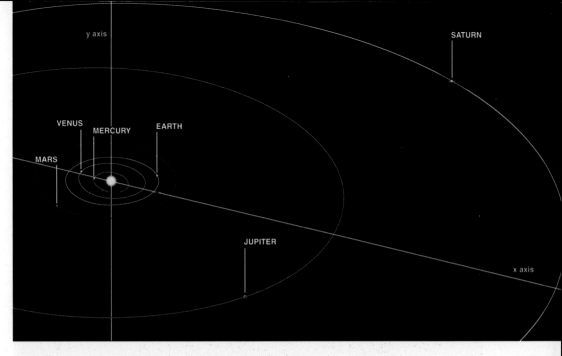

Saturn has one of the longest years in our solar system.

A Saturn Year

A year on any planet is the time it takes to make one orbit around the sun. Because Saturn is so far from the sun, the path it travels is very long. Saturn races through space at almost 22,000 miles (35,400 km) per hour. However, it still takes close to 30 Earth years for the planet to orbit the sun one time. A 60-year-old on Earth would be only 2 years old on Saturn.

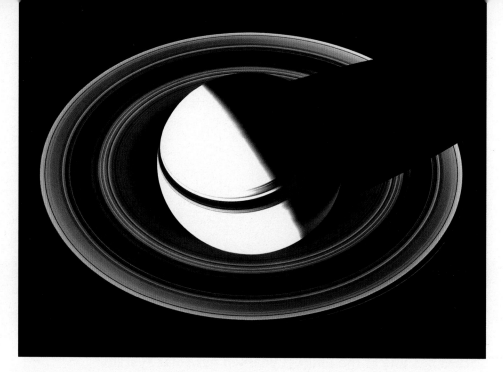

Saturn's rings cast shadows on the day side of the planet. On the night side, the planet casts a shadow on the rings behind it.

A Saturn Day

A year on Saturn is much longer than a year on Earth, but a day is much shorter. Every planet rotates on its **axis**. This rotation creates days on the planet. A day is the time between one noontime and the next. Saturn spins quickly, making one day less than 11 hours long. This is less than half as long as a day on Earth.

Seasons on Saturn

Earth experiences seasons because its axis is tilted. When the North Pole is tilted toward the sun, the Northern **Hemisphere** has summer. The South Pole is tilted toward the sun six months later. Then the Southern Hemisphere has summer.

Saturn's axis is also tilted. Therefore, Saturn also has seasons. Because Saturn's year is so long, the seasons are very long. Imagine a summer that is more than seven Earth years long!

Axial Tilt of Saturn

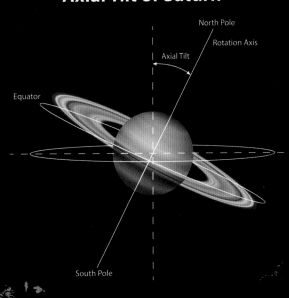

North Pole

Rotation Axis

Axial Tilt

Equator

South Pole

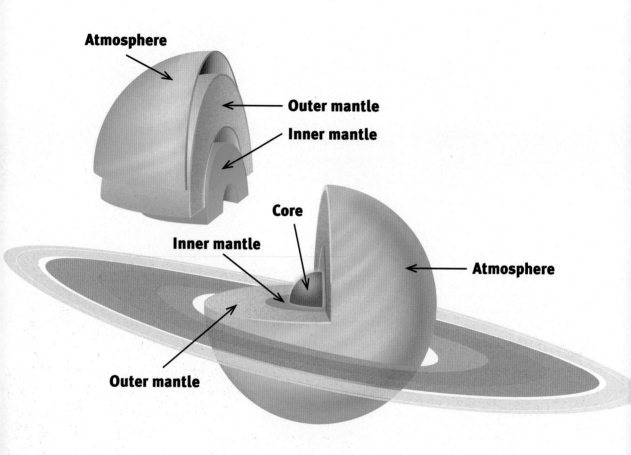

Atmosphere

Outer mantle

Inner mantle

Core

Inner mantle

Atmosphere

Outer mantle

This illustration shows
Saturn's basic layers.

CHAPTER 2

A Gas Giant

Like the other outer planets, Saturn is not solid. Its **atmosphere** is composed mostly of hydrogen, helium, and other gases. Toward the planet's center, the pressure increases. The gases in this **mantle** layer become liquid. Closer to the **core**, the liquid behaves like a metal. It conducts electricity, as metals do on Earth. The core is thought to be made up of iron, nickel, and rock.

Unlike Earth, Saturn has no solid crust.

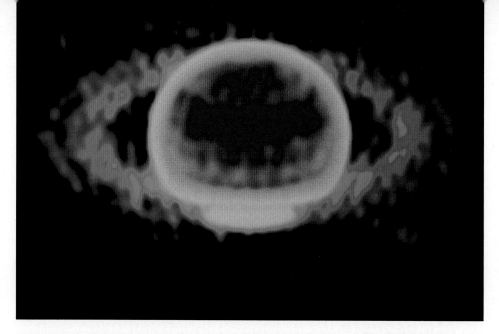

The heat radiating from Saturn is shown in red in this image. The planet's rings reflect some of that heat, showing up in blue.

Hot and Cold

Saturn is a planet of extremes. The temperature at the top of Saturn's clouds can be as low as −280 degrees Fahrenheit (−173 degrees Celsius). The planet's interior, on the other hand, is almost unimaginably hot. Temperatures in the rocky core can reach 21,000°F (11,700°C). This is hotter than the sun's surface. In fact, Saturn releases twice as much heat into space as it receives from the sun.

High Winds

Saturn's cloudy surface is whipped by some of the fastest winds in the solar system. The *Voyager* spacecraft measured winds blowing at more than 1,100 miles (1,770 km) per hour. Like Jupiter, Saturn has colorful bands that can be seen through a telescope. These bands are different layers of clouds. The brighter, higher bands are colder ammonia clouds. Lower down are the warmer, browner ammonia and sulfur clouds.

Saturn's bands may look smooth from a distance, but up close they look more turbulent.

Stormy Weather

With such high winds, it's no surprise that Saturn has its share of storms. Huge thunderstorms occur during the summers. Scientists have also long been studying a gigantic hurricane swirling around the planet's north pole. The eye of the hurricane was 1,250 miles (2,012 km) across. The storm's wind speeds were more than 300 miles per hour (483 kph). Winds in Earth's most powerful hurricanes are only about half that speed.

This image uses false colors to highlight Saturn's clouds. The eye of the polar hurricane is in red. Higher cloud layers are orange or yellow. Saturn's rings appear as bright blue.

In this photo, colors are adjusted to show higher cloud layers (orange) and lower cloud layers (blue).

Bulging Middle

Because it spins so rapidly, Saturn bulges a bit in the middle. This makes it wider than it is tall. If you look at pictures of Saturn, you may see that the planet looks a little bit squashed. In fact, the planet's poles are nearly 3,700 miles (5,955 km) closer to the planet's center than points along Saturn's equator are.

An artist drew this image of the view from Saturn's upper cloud layers. The sun can be seen shining above the rings.

Gravity

Saturn is a much larger planet than Earth. However, its gravity is only a little stronger than Earth's gravity. If your weight on Earth is 100 pounds (45 kilograms), you would weigh 107 pounds on Saturn. This would feel the same as about 49 kilograms on Earth. Of course, you couldn't test this out by standing on Saturn. Saturn is made of liquid and gas. It has no solid surface on which to stand!

Saturn's "Northern Lights"

Saturn has a **magnetic field** that is almost 600 times stronger than Earth's. When charged particles carried by the solar wind strike this field, the result is glowing lights in the sky. These lights are called auroras. They are much like the northern lights here on Earth. As on Earth, these lights are most visible at the north and south poles.

This set of photographs shows charged particles glowing at Saturn's south pole.

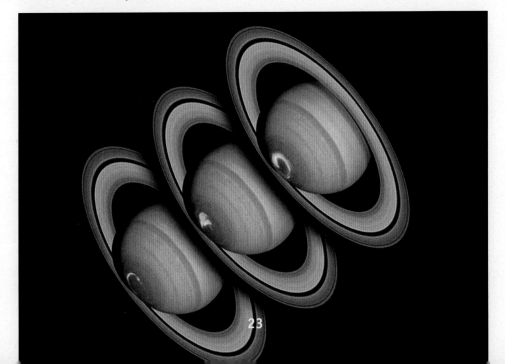

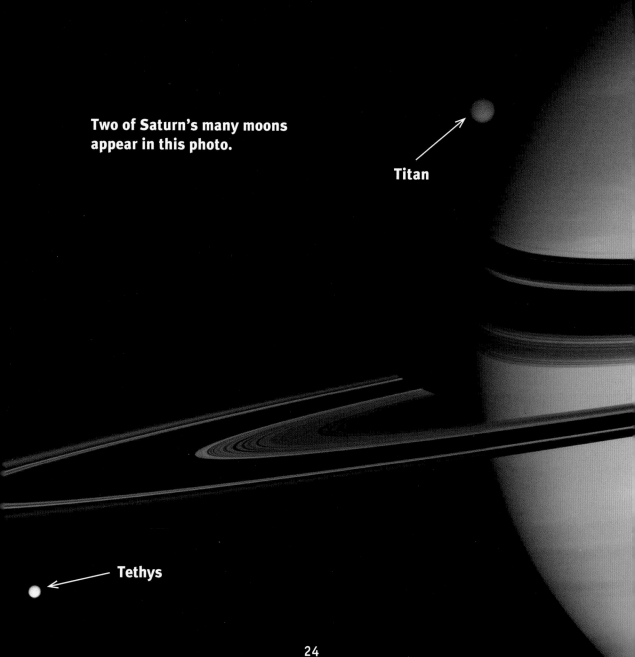

Two of Saturn's many moons appear in this photo.

Titan

Tethys

CHAPTER 3

Saturn's Moons and Rings

Saturn may be best known for the objects that circle it. **Astronomers** have discovered many moons orbiting the planet. In addition to the moons, Saturn boasts a large and beautiful system of rings. The rings extend 175,000 miles (282,000 km) from Saturn's cloud tops. Thanks to their size, they are easy to see through a telescope.

Saturn's rings are almost as wide as the distance between Earth and Earth's moon.

The First of Many Moons

Italian astronomer Galileo Galilei's discovery in 1610 of Jupiter's moons inspired Dutch astronomer Christiaan Huygens. Working with his brother, Huygens built his own telescope and began observing Saturn. On March 25, 1655, Huygens spotted the first and largest of Saturn's moons. He named it Luna Saturni, which means "Saturn's moon." Two hundred years later, astronomer John Herschel changed the name to Titan.

The Huygens spacecraft, named for Christiaan Huygens, landed on Titan in 2005.

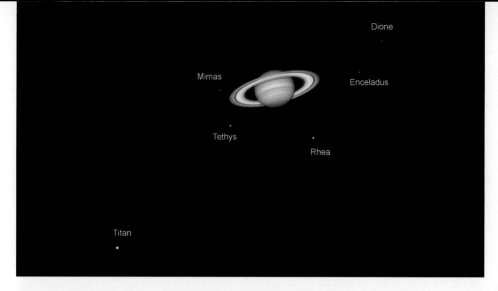

This photo includes six of Saturn's larger moons.

Many More

Italian-born French astronomer Gian Domenico Cassini discovered the next four moons. The discoveries were made from 1671 through 1684. As the design of telescopes improved, it became easier to see objects in space. Over the years, more moons were discovered orbiting Saturn. As of 2013, the count was 62. Most of Saturn's moons are named after gods and giants from Greek and Roman mythology. Others have been named after Norse, Gallic, and Inuit gods.

Titan was named for the Titans in Greek mythology.

Titan's hazy outer atmosphere is highlighted in purple in this photograph. Below this haze is the moon's thick and orange main atmosphere.

Titan

Titan is Saturn's largest moon. It is the second-largest moon in the solar system, after Jupiter's moon Ganymede. Titan measures 3,200 miles (5,150 km) across. It is so large that it affects the orbits of other moons nearby. Titan has a thick atmosphere that is rich in nitrogen. This is similar to what probably existed on Earth before life developed here.

Saturn's Rings

In 1610, Galileo spotted something unusual near Saturn. With his early telescope, he could not tell exactly what he was seeing. His best guess was that Saturn had a smaller planet on either side of it. In 1656, Christiaan Huygens observed the same detail using a more powerful telescope. He realized that Saturn was surrounded by a number of thin rings.

Galileo made many important discoveries about our solar system during his career.

Rings of Ice

Saturn's rings are made up of ice, dust, and debris. Billions of particles compose the rings. The particles range in size from tiny pieces of dust to chunks larger than a house. The rings are very wide, extending thousands of miles from the planet's surface. However, they are also very thin. Some parts of the main rings are only about 30 feet (9 meters) thick.

Saturn's rings may be the remains of a moon that once orbited the planet.

Ice and dust particles sometimes clump together in Saturn's rings.

The colors of Saturn's rings can help scientists figure out what kinds of materials are included in the rings.

How Many Rings?

From far away, it looks as though Saturn has seven or eight wide rings separated by gaps. In reality, those ring groups are made up of hundreds of smaller ringlets. The gaps are created by small moons orbiting within the gaps or by the gravitational pull of moons outside the gaps. Each of Saturn's rings orbits the planet at a different speed!

Disappearing Rings

Galileo first viewed Saturn's rings in 1610. When he looked two years later they had vanished! In another two years, they were back. Galileo concluded that Saturn had "arms" reaching out from its center that grew and disappeared.

November 1999

November 2000

There is a simple explanation: the "arms" are actually rings. Saturn's rings are tilted with its axis. When Saturn's north or south pole is tilted toward Earth, the rings look bright and wide (November 2000, below). When we see the rings edge-on they seem to disappear (August 1995, below). Saturn's rings "disappear" in this way about once every 15 years.

August 1995

October 1998

October 1996

October 1997

In this image, the Greek astronomer Ptolemy is shown being guided by the mythological being Astronomy.

CHAPTER 4

Early Views of Saturn

Because Saturn is easy to see without a telescope, it has been observed since ancient times. No one knows who first discovered Saturn. In 400 BCE, the ancient Greeks named this "wandering star" after their god of agriculture. The first person to look at Saturn through a telescope was Galileo in 1610.

Ancient Greeks thought the planets were stars that moved in unusual patterns. They called them *asteres planetai*, or "wandering stars."

Observing Saturn

The best time to see Saturn is when it is on the same side of the sun as Earth. This position is called opposition. At this time, the sun and Saturn are at opposite sides of the sky, as viewed from Earth. The sun's light shines directly on Saturn, making it look like a bright, glowing disk. Saturn is at opposition once every 378 days.

Powerful telescopes on Earth and in space allow scientists to view more details of Saturn and other objects.

Saturn's Day

Many ancient cultures named the days of the week after gods and objects in the sky. Sunday got its name from the sun, Monday from the moon, and so on. Saturn also contributed its name to a day of the week. It is easy to see Saturn's influence on the English name, as well as that name in other languages. Saturday is *samedi* in French, *Samstag* in German, and *zaterdag* in Dutch.

CHAPTER 5

Exploring Saturn

Pioneer 11 was launched in 1973. It was the first mission to explore Saturn and the outer planets. The spacecraft took six years to reach Saturn, flying past the planet in 1979. On its journey, *Pioneer* discovered a moon orbiting Saturn that had not been observed from Earth. It also spotted a ring that had not been seen before. *Pioneer* is now headed out of our solar system. It carries a plaque with drawings of a man and a woman, in case it is ever found by intelligent life-forms.

Pioneer 11 was active for more than 20 years.

Voyager 1 and 2

Voyager 1 and *Voyager 2* were both launched in 1977. These were the next two spacecraft to visit Saturn. They flew by the ringed planet in 1980 and 1981. Both sent back detailed photos of Saturn and its moons, including several moons that had not been seen before. One of the most interesting discoveries was the thick nitrogen-rich atmosphere of Titan, Saturn's largest moon.

Timeline of Saturn Exploration

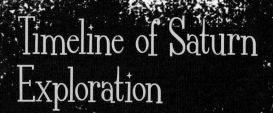

1610
Galileo Galilei becomes the first person to view Saturn through a telescope.

1655
Christiaan Huygens discovers Titan.

Cassini Orbiter

To enter orbit around Saturn in 2004, *Cassini* had to fly between Saturn's rings. The gaps look empty, but they are filled with dust-size particles. *Cassini* recorded more than 100,000 hits from particles in five minutes as it traveled through! *Cassini*'s orbit took it past many of Saturn's moons. A big surprise was the presence of erupting geysers on Enceladus. Scientists had previously thought this moon was frozen and inactive.

1979
Pioneer 11 reaches Saturn. It is the first spacecraft to fly past the planet.

2005
The *Huygens* probe lands on Titan.

2004
Cassini becomes the first spacecraft to orbit Saturn.

The *Huygens* probe landed with the help of parachutes.

The *Huygens* Probe

Cassini carried a small probe designed to explore the surface of Titan. The *Huygens* probe landed on Titan in 2005. It was the first spacecraft to land on a body in the outer solar system. *Huygens* collected information on Titan's atmosphere during its descent. Images showed riverbeds of flowing methane and ethane. After landing, the probe sent back photos showing a flat surface dotted with rounded pebbles. The pebbles are made of frozen water and methane.

Looking to the Future

New missions will explore Titan more. One planned craft would float in Titan's methane and ethane oceans. Another mission would use an orbiting satellite, a balloon, and a lander to study Titan and its atmosphere. In addition to new missions, *Cassini* continues to orbit Saturn. In 2013, the spacecraft captured the first close-up images of Saturn's polar hurricane. They revealed unexpected similarities to Earth's hurricanes. The discoveries do not end there. What will we find out next about Saturn and its moons? ★

Like water on Earth, methane exists as a solid, liquid, and gas on Titan.

This illustration of Titan's surface shows Saturn and the sun through the moon's hazy atmosphere.

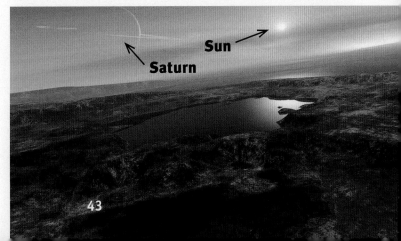

Saturn

Sun

True Statistics

Percent of the total matter of the solar system's planets held by Jupiter and Saturn: 92

Temperature at Saturn's core: 21,000°F (11,700°C)

Number of Saturn days in a Saturn year: 24,525

Number of moons orbiting Saturn: At least 62

Time needed for radio signals to travel from Earth to Saturn: 68 to 84 min.

Distance traveled by *Cassini* to reach Saturn: 2 billion mi. (3.2 billion km)

Did you find the truth?

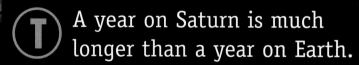

(F) Saturn's moon Titan is the largest moon in the solar system.

(T) A year on Saturn is much longer than a year on Earth.

Resources

Books

Aguilar, David A. *13 Planets: The Latest View of the Solar System*. Washington, DC: National Geographic, 2011.

Owen, Ruth. *Saturn*. New York: Windmill Books, 2014.

Visit this Scholastic Web site for more information on Saturn:
★ www.factsfornow.scholastic.com
Enter the keyword **Saturn**

Important Words

astronomers (uh-STRAH-nuh-muhrz) — scientists who study stars, planets, and space

atmosphere (AT-muhs-feer) — the mixture of gases that surrounds a planet

axis (AK-sis) — an imaginary line through the middle of an object, around which that object spins

core (KOR) — the most inner part of a planet

dense (DENS) — having a large amount of matter packed tightly together

elliptical (i-LIP-tih-kuhl) — in a flat oval shape

hemisphere (HEM-uh-sfeer) — one half of a round object, especially a planet

magnetic field (mag-NET-ik FEELD) — the area around a magnetic object that has the power to attract metals

mantle (MAN-tuhl) — the part of a planet located outside the core

orbit (OR-bit) — to travel in a path around something, especially a planet or the sun

planet (PLAN-it) — a large body orbiting a star

Index

Page numbers in **bold** indicate illustrations

About the Author

Ann O. Squire is a psychologist and an animal behaviorist. Before becoming a writer, she studied the behavior of rats, tropical fish in the Caribbean, and electric fish from central Africa. Her favorite part of being a writer is the chance to learn as much as she can about all sorts of topics. In addition to *Mars*, *Jupiter*, *Mercury*, *Neptune*, and *Saturn*, Squire has written about many different animals, from lemmings to leopards and cicadas to cheetahs. She lives in Long Island City, New York.